Wild
ANIMAL TOWN

Rob Waring, *Series Editor*

HEINLE
CENGAGE Learning

Australia • Brazil • Japan • Korea • Mexico • Singapore • Spain • United Kingdom • United States

Words to Know

This story is set in Zimbabwe [zɪmbɑbweɪ] in southern Africa. It happens in a town called Kariba [kəribə], which is on the Zambezi [zæmbizi] River.

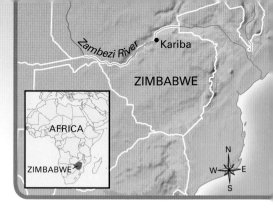

A **Animals of Zimbabwe.** Here are some wild animals you will find in the story. Label the picture with the words in the box.

an antelope	buffaloes	a hippopotamus
a baboon	elephants	a leopard

2. _____

3. _____

1. _____

B Life in the Wild. Read the definitions. Then complete the paragraph with the correct forms of the words.

the bush: a natural area far from towns and cities
game: animals that are hunted for food or sport
herd: a large group of animals of the same type
tame: not wild and not frightened of people
wildlife: animals and plants living independently of people in natural conditions

The (1)_____ that is found in Africa is amazingly varied. The best way to see wild plants and animals is to go out into (2)_____. There, people can often see large (3)_____ of antelope or buffalo. Many people like to see these animals, but they must remember: they're wild, not (4)_____ like animals in a zoo. Unfortunately, many of these wild animals are also (5)_____ animals that people like to hunt.

6. _____

4. _____

5. _____

It's **rush hour**[1] in the town of Kariba. As people hurry off to work or play, they have to remember one important thing: elephants have the **right of way**.[2] Here, in this Zimbabwean town of 30,000 people, there are animals all over!

In Kariba, it's completely normal to see elephants and other wild animals walking down the street. Why? The town was built in a region that used to be a wildlife area. While the town developed and grew, the animals stayed. The people and animals simply got used to each other. Today, Kariba has become a very **civilized**[3] place that shows how humans and animals can live together happily.

---

[1]**rush hour:** the time of day when people are traveling to and from work
[2]**right of way:** the legal right to cross a road before other road users
[3]**civilized:** highly developed; educated

🎧 CD 1, Track 05

Glenn Tatham used to be a **warden**[4] in a national park, and he's lived and worked with animals his whole life. Tatham grew up in Kariba, and says that it's unlike anywhere else on Earth. He explains that what happens in Kariba just doesn't happen in other places. "Kariba has lions, elephants, buffaloes, leopards, all the antelope **species**[5] that occur, [and they're] right up against the town, and in the town," Tatham says. "The fact that elephants are **meandering**[6] through the town, past the schools, past the supermarkets—that's unheard of!"

---

[4]**warden:** a person whose job is to care for a place
[5]**species:** a specific group of living things that have similar characteristics
[6]**meander:** move slowly in no particular direction or with no clear purpose

It's true that wild animals walk around freely in Kariba. It's common to see a herd of buffalo hiding in the trees and bushes that are near the town's streets. The buffalo may not look very dangerous, but when they are bothered, they're some of Africa's most frightening animals. They don't usually live with people, yet here in Kariba they live peacefully right next to humans.

Everywhere in this town, people and animals live together, side by side. On a grassy spot in the town, a group of boys play soccer. Just a few meters behind the boys, hippopotamuses, or 'hippos' for short, swim in a pond. Remember, wild hippos are often very dangerous, and these don't come from a zoo. "These are totally wild, absolutely wild," comments Tatham in amazement as he and the boys stand right next to the pond with the hippos. "These are not in any way or form tame or trained or captured," he adds. "They are completely wild hippos!"

So how did the town of Kariba get like this? The story is an interesting one. The town is fairly new and was established in the late 1950s. It was built as a place to live for people who were working on a huge project nearby. At the time, a **dam**[7] was being built across the Zambezi River to produce **hydroelectric power**.[8]

During the project, the buildings of the town were constructed in the middle of the African bush, an active wildlife area. Why? Because that's where the workers needed to be at the time. However, when the dam was completed years later, the town remained. Since that time, a kind of **tolerance**[9] has developed between man and animal. It has become a living situation that works quite well, but it is one that has certain 'rules'.

---

[7]**dam:** a structure that stops the flow of the river
[8]**hydroelectric power:** power that uses the energy of water
[9]**tolerance:** acceptance of behaviors that are different from one's own

to govern the town. One rule, for example, is that daytime is mainly for people. Tatham explains, "The animals know that [in] the daytime—apart from the baboons and the odd elephant—[they] don't meander amongst the people."

These rules apply to both groups that live in the town. "At nighttime, it's the animals' time," Tatham continues. As night comes, people anxiously return home, and elephants walk into the town center. By midnight, with most of the town asleep, the animals are free to do whatever they want to do.

During the night, the animals sometimes destroy **lawns**[10] and pick up trees. Elephants stand right next to houses and eat the grass and leaves near them. At night, the wild animals seem like they own Kariba as they walk around the town. They don't appear to be troubled by **barking**[11] dogs, or by any people who dare to walk among them.

On dark nights, many humans have run into dangerous situations with the animals. Sometimes they have surprised elephants or other wild creatures, such as buffaloes. This is easy to do when the animal may be standing just a few meters away from the street!

---

[10]**lawn:** an area of grass, usually in front of a house
[11]**bark:** make a loud, sharp noise

Predict

Answer the questions using information you know from reading to this point. Then, check your answers on pages 17 and 18.

1. Have many humans in Kariba been injured by the animals?

2. Why does Glenn Tatham feel sorry for the animals?

3. Where does Tatham usually go at the end of the day?

So just how dangerous is it to live in Kariba? Well, although the animals come out every night in Kariba, there have been very few human injuries or deaths. One of the reasons for this may be the **game corridors**[12] that have been established in the town. These are special areas where animals can move freely through the town and where city development is not allowed. This gives the animals the space they need, and reduces the possibility of man and animal meeting by surprise.

Despite these measures, there will likely be more problems in Kariba. The town is growing, and it's unclear how long these game corridors will remain protected. Tatham finds this very troubling and he says that he actually feels sorry for the animals. "When I look at some of these elephants, who are not so young now, [who were] born in the mid-'40s—as I was—then I can identify with them," he says. He then adds, "[I can identify with them] because they've grown up here, and I've grown up here. It's their home." Tatham feels that the animals of Kariba have a right to stay in their home, just like the people of the town do.

---

[12]**game corridor:** a way or road for animals to travel without being bothered

At the end of each day, when 'rush hour' is over, Tatham often goes down to the lake with his wife to watch the wildlife. As they stand at a safe distance and relax, they smile at the beauty of it all. It's wonderful to be able to see these wild animals in their natural environment.

Tatham knows that his hometown of Kariba has established a slightly uncomfortable balance. However, he also knows that the world is becoming more and more developed every day. Natural lands are being taken away from animals as towns grow. Fortunately, it looks like the the wild animal town of Kariba may have found a balance that works well.

What Do You Think?

1. Would you like to live in Kariba?

2. Why or why not?

3. Will the people and animals of Kariba be able to continue living together for a long time?

After You Read

1. Kariba was _____ a town only for wild animals.
   A. always
   B. once
   C. sometimes
   D. never

2. What view about Kariba is expressed by Glenn Tatham on page 7?
   A. It's hot.
   B. It's attractive.
   C. It's unusual.
   D. It's popular.

3. Which type of animal does NOT live in Kariba?
   A. bear
   B. buffalo
   C. antelope
   D. hippopotamus

4. How does Tatham feel about the living situation in Kariba?
   A. bothered
   B. amazed
   C. confused
   D. frightened

5. In paragraph 1 on page 11, the word 'established' can be replaced by:
   A. grown
   B. progressed
   C. developed
   D. proposed

6. What's a good heading for paragraph 2 on page 11?
   A. Workers Refuse to Leave
   B. Unknown Animals Found
   C. Lawless Place in Bush
   D. People Stay After Project

7. What is the purpose of the rules explained on page 12?
   A. to stop people from seeing baboons
   B. to control the wildlife
   C. to create balance in the town
   D. to give animals freedom

8. What can one find on the streets of Kariba at midnight?
   A. wildlife
   B. tourists
   C. hunters
   D. children

9. Sometimes animals _____ the gardens and homes of people.
   A. improve
   B. damage
   C. surprise
   D. eat

10. The writer probably thinks the town is:
   A. never dangerous
   B. normal
   C. completely lawless
   D. an interesting place

11. Why does Tatham say he feels sorry for the animals?
   A. He thinks that they are unhappy.
   B. He is afraid that they will die soon.
   C. He's worried that they may soon have no place to live.
   D. He feels that the town is not a good place for them.

12. In paragraph 2 on page 18, what does the word 'uncomfortable' mean?
   A. painful
   B. uneasy
   C. useful
   D. quiet

HEINLE Times

REMEMBERING OPERATION NOAH

Almost 50 years after the rescue operation that saved approximately 6,000 animals, the people of Kariba are taking time to remember Operation Noah. It all began with the construction of the Kariba Dam on the Zambezi River in 1956. By the time the dam was finished in 1959, the people who lived in the Zambezi River Valley had moved to higher ground. They wanted to be safe from the water that would build up behind the dam.

However, as the water rose in the valley, it became evident that there was another problem. Thousands of animals were beginning to gather on the tops of hills, which remained dry. Unfortunately, many of these hills soon started to become covered by water. Local game warden Rupert Fothergill started making anxious appeals for money to buy boats and equipment. He and a few helpers had a rough plan to save the animals: they called it 'Operation Noah.'

Operation Noah was not easy to put into action. First, the rescue team had to get to the animals. The tops of trees, which were now underwater, damaged many of the boats. Then, once they reached the terrified animals, the rescuers were often attacked. Some animals, such as snakes and leopards, were extremely dangerous to help. It often took three or more people to save these animals.

In addition to the rescue's safety issues, the rescuers also had to worry about time. They had to work very quickly for two major reasons. First, the waters were rising fast. If they didn't reach the animals quickly, the animals would drown. Second, if a wild animal is held by people for a long time, there's a higher chance that it will die.

Operation Noah Animal Rescue Records

Animal	Number Saved	Number Lost
Antbear	50	2
Baboon	270	2
Black-footed Cat	1	0
Buffalo	88	10
Bush Pig	48	4
Elephant	23	0
Hippopotamus	0	1
Leopard	1	1
Lion	10	0
Monkey	178	6
Night Ape	11	1
Rhinoceros	54	10
Squirrel	6	0
Wildcat	4	0
Zebra	63	17

As people look back and remember this incredible rescue effort, the nearby town of Kariba has a continuing reminder of Operation Noah's success. Many of the animals that were rescued were taken to other places. However, some of the animals stayed in the area, and many of them made the town of Kariba their home.

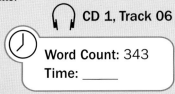

CD 1, Track 06

Word Count: 343
Time: _____

Vocabulary List

antelope (2, 3, 7)
baboon (2, 12)
bark (14)
buffalo (2, 3, 7, 8, 14)
(the) bush (3, 11)
civilized (4)
dam (11)
elephant (2, 4, 7, 12, 14, 17)
game (3)
game corridor (17)
herd (3, 8)
hippopotamus (2, 8)
hydroelectric power (11)
lawn (14)
leopard (2, 7)
meander (7, 12)
right of way (4)
rush hour (4, 18)
species (7)
tame (3, 8)
tolerance (11)
warden (7)
wildlife (3, 4, 11, 18)